Be careful because

Tony Weston

Published 2016
WINWALOE
99, SOUTH STREET,
BRIDPORT,
DORSET,
DT6 3NZ

ISBN 978-1-326-39658-9

A catalogue record for this book
is available from the British Library

Cover image taken from pen and wash
drawing of Sophie

for Sophie

who aged six made us
a card which said

be careful
because be
careful
because
be careful because
I love you

CONTENTS

Be careful because	8
Signature dish	9
You should see yourself	10
Today's lesson	11
Press on	12
Never did	13
In a sieve	14
Skin and bone	15
Finish your veg	16
Forgive me	17
Premature	18
The mind's river	19
Tomorrow doubtless	20
Whoops	21
In Casualty	22
Snapshot	23
Superbounce	24
Vanishing in the steam/ This plate	25
Days later	26
Insert this	27
A poor hand	28
A fresh light	29
For Felix	30
Stamping ground	31
But who?/ Fifty-two years	32
Returning to your fall	33
Tissue song	34
Thistledown	35
Waiting for the weather	36
Angel dream	37
No safe beaches	38
Angel nature notes	39
Result	40
Keep half an eye?	41
Birthday poem	42
You can put your hand down now	44
Chloe's Lyric Concert	45

Finding Physio	47
Discrete images	48
Timing is everything	49
Rant	50
Maker	51
A young man sees the future	52
Pah!	53
One quick crack/But half a sonnet	54
Centenary/ Our glorious past	55
Kingdom Come	57
Pencil on a piece of string	58
Making an exhibition	59
A lesson remembered	60
Morning song	61
Night sweats	62
Triangle of forces	63
Our mark	64
Good paint	65
Night- night my little darling	66
Mental shrug	67
Mother-daughter	68
Press any key	69
Insight	70
Plea	71
Whose Angel are you?	72
I don't need this	73
How to kill a good man	74
People who can't compromise	75
Symbiosis	76
Pretend	77
Forbidden fruit	78
Rude awakening	79
Mr. Weston's Book	80
Love watching	81
Scottish Wednesday	82
Lemons in a bag	83
Eyewash	84
Earwash	85
A nod in passing	86

Vegetarian section 87
Shoe song 88
I hear you 89
Drop everything 90
Incongruity 91
What's wrong with poems? 92
To make a little something 93
Angel in trouble 94
Carwatch 95
Telescope 96
Supervision 97
Curtains for us 98
A time to celebrate? 99
Winging the moment 100
Nearly perfect 101
Staying with us 102

Be careful because

Be careful because

I listen to her ansaphone which lets me know
she isn't there. I wonder what has slipped my mind?
What has not registered? Occasionally she'll laugh
and say *it's boys—they never listen* and then

her nine-year old will eyeball her on my behalf—
but just suppose something *is* wrong? A day
gone bad, the bloody ME put her in her bed?
Should I go down and walk the dogs—only

to interrupt her trying to teach the boy,
to get him just to write her half a page?
She'll not be pleased. We'll have a coffee then—
I ask her mother does she know? I ring again.

I listen to her ansaphone which lets me know
she is not there because, *maybe, she is helping*
someone to the longest lashes in the world—twice told
and hearing this, I'm sold—I want some too.

Signature dish

Being chef du jour I do my best to prep ahead.
Before I go to play my tennis fours I've halved
tomatoes, the nice big sort that smell of
summer in an old greenhouse, a little sugar,
pepper, salt, a douse of olive oil, a sprinkling
of fresh thyme—into the Rayburn top back shelf.
New potatoes next, cabbage to steam on top,
plates in the bottom oven, except the boy's— he
cannot bear things hot. Last off it's salad, sliced
orange, chicory, left as yet undressed.

I play quite well, for me at least. Before I shower
I check the tomatoes—looking good. I lay
the table, take out the veggie sausages to thaw.
Towelled, changed, refreshed I make a start
on the boy's unheated plate. Cucumber eyes,
new moons of apple for the hair, cashews
for eyebrows—cabbage for cheeks. Sausage
for moustache, potato nose and beard will come
when cooked, along with ketchup for the lips.
I dress the salad as they severally arrive,
turn on the water jug, and fill the rings—
no that's not right, the wrong way round.
This all looks beautiful they say at once beginning
to get in the way. It'll be ten minutes, I scowl.
The boy scoots off, old Beano bound.
His mum puts lemon in the water jug.
Her mum is telling how little the collection
was despite a goodly number there.
I'm keeping calm and carrying on

In the kitchen women come and go
talking of stuff I do not need to know
and indeed there will be time....

The meal is splendid, I'm duly chuffed.

That evening, on my way to bed, of course
I do remember them—my precious tomatoes
top back shelf. I carry them outside to hiss
on the cold stone, my signature-in-charcoal-dish.

You should see yourself

My lovely Grandpa shaved cut-throat;
the leather strop, sun-sharpened blade
his thumb with that thin line of blood.
As you get older, boy, the skin gets thin.
For me a safer tool for trial by blade
and glass. Thing is, the verdict's not
yet in. Let's say—I judge myself
grown old disposable in hand. You
should see yourself, my women laugh.
They mean it kindly, so they say. Well,
I've seen myself take pains to shave
and grow like to my Grandpa, though
not quite—and oddly there are days when,
leaning back, I catch my mother's face
concerned behind the spattered glass.

Today's lesson

Let's see. We wanted Africa.
We wanted slaves, we wanted gold.
We wanted timber, we struck oil.
We traded hard and took our losses too—
and don't you see they got the best of it— we
gave them our Democracy? Too bad a few
young chicks must pay the extra on the deal.
So, the big man in Ajuba sits and nods
and weighs his smiles like any village chief
and the big man in America inveighs
against this uncivilised outrage.

Bokoharam, we're the boys,
don't give a damn
in our stolen Scorpions
Bokoharam

Who gave them drugs, who gave them guns,
who gave them Allah on a chain? Christ knows.
Let's see, let me explain. God made us in his image,
right and gifted us dominion? So, no surprise
we thought them cattle without souls.
It must be said, they sold themselves. So look,
these animals in tremor round the armoured car,
these boys with AK's calling on their God, know
what they're at. School's over—let the girls be sold.

Bokoharam, we're the boys,
don't give a damn
in our stolen Scorpions
Bokoharam

Press on

Hopeful are we sneers the Angel—
turn the thing on and posit or pray that
the Infinite Monkey is gibbering inside?
I might have thought if I could
once lower myself to thought
you'd do better to sit and stare
at your hands they've lived at least
maladroit creatures that they are
I stare at my hands— I generally do
what Angels say—the odd thing is
I've never seen before how different
the two palms are the right more
wrinkled with perhaps a faint whiff
of resentment Martha and Mary
the Angel prompts in my ear
and now I look it's true my left
has a slightly contemplative air
the fingers are a touch longer too
and the palm less troubled by day
to day wear I rub them together
and look again sure all such nonsense
must disappear the right hand goes
to my nose like a child seeking comfort
the left drums on the desk in disgust
then pulls a fresh tissue from the box
press on says the Angel press on

Never did

You see the difficulty
the Angel says
you're not the one thing
nor the other—you disappear
into the crack between—
you have the arrogance
but not the self-belief
though this is not unknown
of course this way you have
of drawing back short
of some mastery as if to say—
this isn't really me I could
do this and yet I can't since
then I would be noticed
indeed understood as
really bad or even good as
really dark or even light—
but why O why spend all
your little might on this?

Sadly I smile— I don't
believe in Angels— never did

In a sieve

The early sun shows what we're made of—dust
and how the spiders have been expertly industrious
beyond the perspex and the glass. Secondary glazing
can keep in some warmth some comforting it seems
but still the sun will show the shedding of our skin
and leave us standing naked before God or all the vast
not-God we cannot see although we scream
a billion quarks round costly tunnels in the ground—

and if by looking for the heart of things sidelong
this yields a thousand sparks invisible hung for dear life
feet hooked hands clawed like animals under lorries
and fast trains who would and should have drowned—
what were they thinking of to act like this to leave
their known worlds far behind? We've nothing for them.
The Government will keep us from our consciences
the poverty of soul they bring. They went to sea in a sieve.

Skin and bone

We are all of us skin and bone
though some of us hide it better
it's wonderful what you can do
given carbs and a banker's letter

with our rockets and guns and bombs
we are proud of our status quo
nobody spoils our fun
nobody we might know

the World is a soft boiled egg
we're just about to tee off
we're after a cosmic hole in one
there'll be nobody by to scoff

it's marvellous what we've achieved
look how we're chasing the stars
they say from out there in space
you can see the pretty scars

we're too grown-up for Heaven
we're too clever by half for Hell
we are all of us skin and bone
though some of us hide it well

Finish your veg

He sits his back against the wall, on the funny stool
that Grandpa made before his mummy was even born.

Her back is to the garden and the sun and, as he pokes
his tandemed straw through the small, soft windows

in the seedy slice he feels her frown as if the sun went in.
He puts it down and eats a carrot eyebrow. Cucumber

was for eyes with half a strawberry on each one. Carrot
made the nose and underneath a bristly cashew moustache.

He ate this first. The hair is apple in half-moons. The cheeks
are cheesy things in breadcrumbs, the cheese all runny

as you cut in with your knife. Below the ketchup lips a beard
of small potatoes but that's all gone. His two-straw swings

like a tall crane from his far glass towards his mouth.
He sips. He does not risk a blow of bubbles back, but picks

the stained-glass slice and tries again. *Felix!* says Grandmama.
He takes a bite. Not really hungry anymore, he knows there's

still the cabbage and the carrot left and two spare eyes—
without the strawberries. The grown-ups have all finished.

Like wolves they sit around him, growling one by one.
There could be strawberries and cream, snarls Grandpa Wolf.

Forgive me

Forgive me but it's hard to judge
the knife the car the gun in Santa Barbara
were not to blame— that soul-locked boy
had held his cry in just too long
he only wanted to be loved

forgive me if I smile

she on the other hand *had* loved
successfully but oh so shamefully *made*
in Lahore what other option for the bricks?
The whore had stained her family inside
and out the Court could not ignore

forgive me if I shrug

Okay to the four-square guys with tattooed 2nd
Amendment on their chests the crime was not
to do with guns as such but knives and cars
and while they sympathise
their goddam Culture is at stake

forgive me if I sigh

at evidence just brought to Court—
the family of the Lahore girl was forced to kill
a sister for the self-same crime and he the man
had strangled his first wife to marry this one
with retrospective blessing from her son

forgive me if I laugh

forgive or not it's hard to judge
what love might have to do with Laws—
boys kick computer tarts to death
real girls kick in the mango trees
it's knowing which is preferable

forgive me if I weep?

Premature?

As when the over-cautious soul
cuts engines, throws the fenders out
and loses way before it's time

so that the line that's thrown falls back
into the dark between where shadows
lurk and drift and flit and O, too wide

to step across, a leap it dare not take—
but, looking down, a face stares up
and winks an eye and blows a kiss

as shoes and socks and shirt
and all the rest drop down to lie
like stepping stones across the dark—
as with a green sigh you let go.

The mind's river

Suppose you herd them
with your special stick
the floating empties of your
bubbled days knot them
together with some string
a plank or two across
another for a paddle

and so set out against
the muddy slow
polluted stream
ignoring all
the troubling debris
floating down
the horrid objects surfacing

and barely for a moment
at the childhood island
step ashore but
pushing on regardless
as the waters run more
urgent now and clear so
you must wade them

as your flesh falls numb
until you stumble clear
to lie face cloudward on
the chalky hill
and with your fingers part
the butterflies above the grass
from whence your soul is issuing

Tomorrow doubtless

Some illegal, new-come Sun has scoured
night's teflon from the sky, not knowing,
in this country, this is wrong. We like it grey,
a wipe with kitchen roll is all it needs.
Poor eager fool, she's left no trace of cloud,
of vapour trail. She wants so much
to do it right—and so stands out. Alas, she
will be caught and shipped back East.
Tomorrow, doubtless, comes another Sun.
Downstairs there's little sign of her—except
where she has dabbed the kitchen floor
with golden light but left the crumbs. Outside
in the yard the crocuses stand polished and alert
and in the air a scent of woman sweet and clean.
Perhaps I'll keep her safe under the stairs?

I shake my head and go back in to wonder
if the day will ever dull again? You'll bus
the boy into the Keep in Dorchester. I'll drive
his Ma her frightening unknown road.
The two of us will climb the scaffold come the noon.
Sounds serious I know—I dramatise— my daughter's
chimney's letting in the rain. Ah, in life's game
you don't get children without pain. Don't stir—
I kiss the thought of you until we kiss again.

Whoops

Sat upstairs in my bedroom I
think I hear you call—so, step out
on the landing, saying,
Did you call? No, no. No,
it's nothing. Are you sure?
Yes, no—nothing at all. So,
instead of coming down to see
the way I should have done,
I go back to my poems
and plough quietly on.

The phone, an hour later, snaps
my thread. You don't pick up
so I assume you're playing
in your garden. I get it just before
the ansaphone. *Darling,* you say,
calm as a peony on a summer day,
I'm sitting in the car park
and I think I've broken my wrist.
Where? I ask, recovering my wits.
You'll see me just as you drive in.
The paramedic's here. Darling,
I'm shouting now— I've no idea
where you are. Which car park?
I left a note. You sound aggrieved—
for one long moment I think you're
going to make me guess— *at*
Morrisons, you say. *I'd like*
some Ibuprofen and some Arnica.

In casualty

It's quicker so I drive you there myself.
You're white as paper, busy telling me
how lovely everyone has been—the couple
in the motorcycle gear, the paramedic
who was quickly there, how it was just this
little kerb, how you were in a skipping mood.

There is a space. I park the car and join you
back inside. Eventually they take a look.
We wait again. Time does that thing
of stretching out like bubble gum. We stare
at it, its flavour almost gone. Finally we
each take a bit and swallow it. X-ray next.
They say they'll give you gas and air
before they try to pull it straight. Lovely
you say, I remember having *that*—from
Sophie, when my child was born.
The trouble is the cylinder is duff
or empty, the replacement lacking
the knob to turn it on. While this is
sorted the Doctor and the nurses
come and go like waves discussing pebbles
on a beach. I stand the while and hold
your other hand. At last they fill your wrist
with anæsthetic and he bends and yanks
and pulls, you smile as if it's just a game.
It doesn't hurt you say—it doesn't hurt.

Snapshot

Bound for infinity the cracks between the kitchen
quarry-tiles soar out through the open doors
through the coloured garden and the grey stone wall
and press on through the hill you always thought was home,

through Flanders where the thousands died, Warsaw,
Manchuria where the millions were displaced, Quebec,
and back barely delayed by Cornwall's white clay pits
and through Devon's bloody soil and through the chalk

and through my shoulder blades all in the space of half
a breath—you in your too appropriate summer dress,
dead-heading things back into life, your plastered fist
stuffed full of leaves with insect egglets underneath.

Superbounce

We're in the garden. Sitting in the sun.
The boy is being good. He loves his Grandmama.
Full of solicitude, he offers her his bouncy ball.
She laughs and tells him, thank you, no.
He goes to bounce it for her in the hall.
It's what you need, a wall to bounce a ball against.
It means you've half the time to think. Wooden bat,
ball worn bare of fluff, it was enough, back then.
It makes you quick and agile, hones the eye—so says
the old boy to himself, watching his grandson bounce
the little sphere in the confines of the tiled hall. Thing is
the ball, freed from its plastic pack, is going mad.
Too full of bounce, too unpredictable, it hurls itself
from floor to ceiling, ricocheting past the old boy's ear
like a demented fly—no stopping it, no swotting it.
He tries. A little while he tries and fails. The child
though, is full of glee and sometimes manages.
He too is full of superbounce. Briefly his hyper-
Universe and the old man's are parallel and
moments now they touch, but he can see how,
even as he watches, they detach and tear away.
So, what's new? Why everything. Before I'm dead,
he tells himself, as the hyper-active ball topples
another ornament, this grown blithe boy will have
a flashcard for a brain and store his precious,
circling soul somewhere in the pop-upped sky.

Vanishing in the steam

Before the shower steams up I see him eyeing me
from round the corner of the shelves on which
we keep the tissue-salts the ibuprofen and elastoplasts.
I think he must be thinking what's become of me
this boy who's sketching as he looks and wondering how
to lose the four-stone and the fifty years and then
I realise just as he disappears he cannot see me   from
the bright right eye that takes me in— because it's gone.

This plate

This plate I cosset like a damaged child,
I fish now from the dishwasher (too cruel)
to wash by hand. The line of glue still holds.
When I first made it long ago this blue whirled
plate such pots were easy come and easy go
just one of several spares made to a set.
We kept the six for our own use and every day
for twenty years they've been our friends.
Now three are left to us and this cracked one
I dropped a year ago and carefully glued
and make a point of daily using it. I'd hate to
think it felt I thought the less of it—
this plate I cosset like a damaged child.

Days later

The Consultant is appalled. He stares
at his computer screen as if at some
catastrophe that's going viral. He turns
it round so we can share his view.
This is terrible, we'll have to have you in
and operate—some time next week.
Feebly we protest— it's mending now?
Well if you want a hand that finishes like this—
he makes like a darts-player with his wrist.
Late in the day he tries to reassure,
but warns it never will be really right.

We walk away. We'd like to walk away.
We'd like to walk away to that
far place before you didn't think
and didn't look and didn't lift your foot.

Insert this

I should have written this back then
but being too busy being Superman
catching the daily bullet between my teeth
(it passes belief how much there is to do
when your woman takes unwelcome breaks)
it passed me by as in a blur. Suffice to say the
surgeons briefed us on the morning
of the op and I recall you after on the ward
and only just come round being so concerned
for the woman opposite who called and called
won't someone help me, won't someone, please? and
when I went for water I recall how the nurses
smiled each time I said your name. I recall
or do I remember you? You telling me one
week later how the surgeons came and stood
like naughty boys confessing how your wrist
was really difficult—how they enjoyed
the tricky bits, how smug they looked,
big black Martin, thin white Mr.Crook.

A poor hand

Taking our shower together—ah, what fun—
your plastered arm wrapped tight in cling film,
cringing close until the hot comes through,

we use shampoo to soap you trying not to hurt.
Part of me delights in this—the nearness
and your need of this sadly unpractised

tenderness. I find it hard to turban right
the towel round your head, though towelling
what you cannot reach, this I can do, though

combing out your hair's another thing.
It takes a wincing while to get the knack.
Our daughter gives us stuff to rub in first

then we discover vinegar. This rigmarole
goes on for weeks—we laugh and swear,
for you it's hard as hell to bear—for me, truth told,
my love, I'd not have missed it for the world.

A fresh light

Today he came with his black dog.
It's just a pup—goes flying round the room
then straight in for the crotch. Well,
I wouldn't mind, he's really very sweet
it's just with no pyjamas on, you know?
The Angel calls him Dawkins—Dawkins?
Makes a joke of it—*you should hear me*
squawking Dawkins! Dawkins—settle down.
Dawkins sits and tilts his neat black head
and looks at us. The Angel breaks him off
a piece of chocolate and little Dawkins begs.
Chocolate is bad for dogs! The Angel laughs.
Chocolate is bad for everyone—that is the point
of chocolate—oh, never fear, Dawkins is immortal,
quite unkillable. Would you like to hear him talk?
Give over. Dogs can't talk. You can't talk,
can you boy? Dawkins wags his tail and tilts
again in affirmation of this negative.
Well, admits the Angel, *not talk perhaps— it's*
more a kind of plainsong lilt. Dawkins! Speak to us
of God. At first I can't quite make it out
but then my ear adjusts. *There's nothing there,*
chants the Angel's little dog, *there's not*
the slightest whiff—therefore God cannot exist.

For Felix

Small ginger cat
big golden soul
you called her Honey
and untold the many
joys she caught and left
for you inside the propped
door of your heart.
Though her last spoon now
is licked feel how her claws
climb up your shirt
to bring her purr
next to your ear.

Stamping ground

We see him most days every week
but still we are his holiday.

His duvet folded to a sleeping bag.
we find him fast-off on the floor,

face in the carpet, thumb in mouth.
I lay a pillow there for him

and put myself at last to bed.
Later, going for a pee,

he hasn't moved and yet
the pillow's underneath his head.

Exquisite there he lies,
this treasure of our latter days.

The fact he's being bloody
to his mother isn't fair—but then

she is his stamping ground,
his day to day and always there.

But who?

We are stuck with it now and it's not so bad
though I know in his heart he wants a dad
not a Grandpa—but who to shoe into that spot
his father no more than a distant blot
he fears will come and steal him away
one terrible trampolining day?
So it's me he thumps or hugs or takes for his cue
as to what it is a man must do—
we are stuck with it now and it holds much joy
for both of us—though he is not my boy.

Fifty-two years

Our Anniversary is coming up as
always I feel guilty in advance
guilt peppered with resentment
that I will not find a present apropos
a way to celebrate the two of us
and as always think each day
together unselfconsciously we light
and blow each other's candle gently out
yet do not make a thing of this
but close our eyes and breathe and wish.

Returning to your fall

You want it gone the blue cast on your wrist
which we agree is mending now how else
would you be cutting with a knife albeit only
soft red peppers swimming in their sauce.

Twelve days to go that's all and your bleached arm
will wave as naked as a babe born to a beach
go carefully my love bent double there dead-heading
everything in sight as if your life and so it does.

I watch you trip and right yourself your good hand
full of stuff you see me watching *I'm being careful*
I really am it isn't fair you say returning to your fall
I was just feeling happy I skipped a kerb that's all.

Tissue song

It may be fancy, but I fancy as a cold kicks in
and you are thick with it, it thins the skin—

not just beneath the nose, around the lips,
toes too get rubbed, start blistering. Hips,

shoulders also start to ache. The knee
we paid to have so quickly done

is catch and grind once more. Hello pain,
it must be months? Bumping into you

I'm wondering, full circle or square one?
Excuse me while I sneeze—life—

must go on— I fancy as— a cold kicks in
and on—and on—that's better—on!

Thistledown

In the bottom right quadrant of the lower pane
of my sash window raised against
the summer heat
a spider's web you cannot see but for this piece
of thistledown which dances to the breath
of early cars—
inconsequential frail device for carrying on
its line of life now uselessly suspended in
another's thrall
I listen for the sound of tiny swearing
at such catastrophe

So in the lower quadrant of my right eye
the cancer lodged and cost me much
but left behind
a piece of consequential thistledown
still hanging there against the day the rains
swipe down—
there is no sound of swearing now
the fit has passed just silent webs
of words to hang
below to catch the eye of those
on holiday or back with bags
of stuff to eat

Waiting for the weather

Gaza—what can you do? Helplessly we shrug
flaky on the rights and wrongs
though reason says sledgehammer/nut

instinctively we mute the sound— try not to see
the images of people much like us
torn jeans and bloody scrabbling fists

or any useless thing to lift the concrete beam
crushing a neighbour's child's legs—
and if we could we would cry out to warn

the young man calling standing staring round—
of course we've seen it all a hundred times—
a step another step he falls a sniper's grimace

defines the gravity of his trespass and since
we mute the silent screams we miss
the first part of the weather when it comes—

it seems the heat goes on oppressively though
for the days ahead a flashing icon shows
some comic lightning and suggests the crump

of thunder— I substitute the roistering tanks
the blatant swinging of their guns—
the arc of hopeful rockets from the ruins

Angel dream

This is new—
I have once from my waking corner eye
seen my Angel speaking with another
but their tongue meant nothing to me
more than the scratch of feathers
on rough stone

but in my dream
translation comes *Why do you stick*
with him—don't you feel groans the other
ashamed— what makes you think him
worth the time and trouble?
Time I have

laughs my Angel
soon enough he will be dust
for now he interests me— I see the other
snort with glee a line of silver snot
falls from him to the ground
becomes a snake

behave yourself
scolds my Angel *can't you see*
he's watching us? No way says the other
dead to the world dead to pretty well
everything ask me— this is too much
I roll over in my dream

and catch the snot-snake by the tail
and swallow it *oh, dear* says my Angel
you've done it now—I'm not sure which of us
he means— the other Angel flaps toward me
as I scream

No safe beaches

The sea of Time has no safe beaches
no place between two flags to swim
tides might seem poised as

yet unturned but sideways
rips may bear away
at any moment those we love

ah yes also we love this sea
our oldest bravest enemy
time out of mind

under our feet
the pebbles
suck and run

Angel nature notes

This is Man. He looks for patterns
sees the hand of God in raindrops
and the splat of flies across
the windscreen of his car

the fact that with each swerve
of his the pattern is reshaped
seems never to occur to him.
Homo oblivious—alas no Angel—

sublimely blind to consequence
and yes there was a time
before we took the bungee jump
before He took his penknife out—

don't dwell on this—yes what we were
looks down on us but we
still know them for the cowards
they everlasting are.

This is Man—for all his stupid coping
ways— much more akin to us—
we watch his generated days
with sadness and with hope.

Result

It so happens I have one here
says the Angel I don't look up
I know his little games *catch*
it hits me just below the ear
I look up now mid-swear

he's nowhere to be seen
the scroll is fastened with
a thread of golden hair
intrigued I slide it off

AWARD FOR A LIFE
    Spent failing
This certificate is given
in recognition of a lifetime
devoted to drawing back—
not that old thing
. . . .
several rows of dots
for me to put my own words in.
I roll it up again and though I search
I cannot find the golden tie
my own hair is not long enough.
I shove the damn thing
in the drawer I use
for competition entry forms

I load my crossbow
with my favourite pen
and wait the whistling of wings.

Keep half an eye?

Are you on, says the Angel
on what I wonder?
you'll keep half an eye?
with my good eye I take him in.
keep the home fires burning?

Thing is I tell him this week's
a bit busy visitors three lots
and today I'm down to help
the wife set up the tables
for the Quaker's Tea Party
in the Peace Garden—

thing is says the Angel
not listening as per *I've got*
three Megas on my plate
well underneath my wing—

then there's my tennis I say
if my knees can stand it
if one doesn't show
it ruins the game
it's a question of numbers—

Syria Gaza Kurdish-Iraq don't
tell me you haven't clocked
what the fuck is going on?

I don't like his tone
Look I say pass me a peg
I'm hanging our smalls
out on the line you must
have heard what happened
to my wife there's a limit
to what a man can handle
38 degrees won't let me be
fatigue you know sets in

All I'm asking he says—
all you're asking is more
than a body can stand
All I'm asking he yells
declining out of sight
is you keep half an eye—
on your own sad sodding soul

Birthday poem

I've taken to it like a natural:
I wear the decent shirts of dead men—
or should that be the shirts of decent—
be that as it may, today's blue rounded
collar job with stiffeners looks okay,
appropriate to this restaurant as though
I were a broker here on holiday.
My party all on best behaviour
wife, daughter, daughter's lovely boy

coping well pretending that he likes
the place, surprised to find the chef's
own little pumpkin-seeded rolls
are edible dipped in the oil and vinegar.
As usual I eat too much too fast
and, finished first, watch the people
I best love enjoy each other's drollery.

Later, we walk it off along the beach.
The boy and I take to the dunes of stones
heaped massively along the promenade
in lieu of what was ripped away last year.
Out in the steel-ruled surf black-rubbered
boys paddle fluorescent boards far out
to catch the waves—high-fiving, falling as
they pass. They must be mad and cold.
My grandson hurls himself in imitation
down the pebbled slopes and lies akimbo
staring at the winter sky—*You try it Grandpa.*
Knowing I'm really much too stiff and grand
give me your hand, I say, and haul him up
and off he dives again. There are still things
that I might do for him and stuff that he
will do for both of us. We load his new-bought
boots with stones with magic holes.

You can put your hand down now

Tonight you will not have to sleep
with your arm suspended in its
clumsy purple sleeve of sponge and
though I worry that such licence won
may have you turning on your fist
I am reminded it's *your* hand.
So now I must undo your ad hoc
mid-air ball and chain and soon
no doubt you will shake off my
guiding arm and next you're out
there gardening and when I tell you
you must stop you'll laugh and scold
at my temerity and I shall go indoors to
sulk and feel another cold sore pricking in.

.

Chloe's Lyric Concert

The night this Mermaid
sitting just in front
flicked back her hair
into my drink
was full of such unlooked
epiphanies and though

we left before the dancing—
carrying away
my sore shoulder
your mending wrist

this being our privilege

to leave the songbird
with her emptied spoons
her eyes still dancing in her skull
the catererer in her body
totting up

to leave Bobie's Gurlz
with one coy ukelele glance

our privilege

to leave those dancing girls
still speculating who has won
the piercing and just where
they'll have it done

and funny Nikki
with her bright lost eyes
hiding somewhere in the stables
with the frightened horses
nuzzling her padded bra—

out in the night
you clutch my hand

our privilege

despite the who or what
that scuttles down the street
ahead of us that turns
and growls into the dark
that also would not stay to dance

that howls its pain.

Finding Physio

Finding Physio we trawl the magazines.
You say you doubt you'll ever drive again.
I tell you how just now I saw this bloke

in a pickup truck back out with just
his blued-up arm, his other busy
with the phone—you're not impressed.

I sit beside you and can hear your fingers catch
as you flex-unflex your mended hand.
Despite the full up corridor the Physio is calm

and has the time for idle chat. She says
you're doing well but when she calibrates
your grip your face falls like a little stone.

She gives you things to do at home, some
squeezy mastic in a plastic water cup.
She's most encouraging and kind.

I know although you laugh and smile
that none of this has happened
will happen—is really happening.

Discrete images

Last night
in the late sun
the light on your small hill
evoked a cup cake
one might lift
in a quiet garden room
with thank-yous
from a gentil plate

This morning early
it's less cake
than baby's bum
and fists of careful
cotton wool poised
efficiently to wipe—

Alas alas
I missed the heaped
teaspoon of sugar
and the giving
of the breast

Timing is everything

They walk their kids along beneath the cliff
the blown air bastes their beetroot backs
they carry folding chairs towards the shade
and in another time perhaps not this the shale
will sigh and slump and bury them their lungs
will burst their hearts will stop it will be quick
the cliff is dancing to a different beat slow slow
quick quick slow though unaware of this they shout
their little ones to wait—*You know the sea is dangerous!*

We sit our bottoms on an upturned boat and start
to read the pebbles at our feet un-numbering them
to know their thoughts these secret handmaids
of the sea who fathom things the cliff does not
the sea in turn acknowledges the lifting moon
the moon a make-up mirror to the fading star
lost to all sense of when her tiny universe began
and if it's *now* to step into the falling black
and how to take the curtain-call.

Rant

One old man he writes verse
his old rhymes get worse and worser
with a comma here and a colon there
he really thinks one ought to care
he cannot see where this will end
where the full-stop sits for his poor friend
with a knick knack paddy whack
give a dog a bone transplant or two
and send him home
soon he'll stop moving
soon he'll lie still
under the shadow of this sweet hill
or perhaps we will shake him
like wicked pepper
under the noses
of those who knew better

The Oncologist says
Well at least we tried
he had a chance till his marrow fried
we did all we could but the poor sod died
he lifts his glass as he waits for his dinner
I really thought we were onto a winner
I'd have done the same in his sad shoes
life is a battle we're born to lose
but one must fight while there is breath
to batten the hatches down against death—
do you think I like it the smell of failure?
It's just how it is how it has to be—
infection drifts in with every dahlia.

Maker

I used to say, when I was making pots,
when I was standing on that wind-blown stall,
when people asked me why, why sell your work
so cheap? *Look, you have to shift the stuff*
or else the urge to make it goes. Oh, yes, I'd nod,
if you're Van Gogh, who hardly sold a thing,
if you're a total loser such as that,
who paints more real than life,
whose yellow fever holds you fast,
why then you need a brother
a doctor and a field of crows—
a loaded gun.

Of course, my buyers have long walked away.
Sometimes I used to shrug the idiot and wrap
the mug/ teapot like a mute. There were odd days
God knows, I managed lightness and a little charm –
and cleared the stall. The joy such days of packing up!
I couldn't wait to get back to the wheel and kiln.
Look, here's the thing I meant to say. God knows
He's made too many of us now. He marks us low,
sends crates to Funfairs round the world,
for little boys to practice their Kalashnikovs.
Or crates them up in leaky
boats and watches as they drift
away.One day, of course,
he'll just walk off
and leave us all
in cardboard boxes
in the rain.

A young man sees the future

You solve the things you can
if you've got any sense those things
that are beyond you – let them go

Across the street
I watch him now
this old fool barefoot
in his dressing gown
taking his yale-lock apart
his hair's too long his sight
too shot for such neat work
I want to tell him that
his door's not warped as such
from summer sun as dropped
and that is why the tongue
no longer slides into the catch

I see him break off matches
to pack the screw holes
cutting card to pack it out
he should just pack it in

If I could simply cross
the years between
and take the tools
from his old fists

but as it is you have to learn—
you solve the things you can

Pah!

Where do they go the lost tools
the ones you knew you had last time
for doing something down the road
you know you didn't leave them there—
someone would have mentioned it?

Somewhere is a garden shed
old door not rotten at the foot
and glass that hasn't slipped
where rows of oiled and polished tools
are clipped around the walls
and leap like greyhounds to the hand—

or is that Heaven?

Back on solid ground—
as you get on it's not so much
the memory evaporates as all
the cardboard boxes stacked inside
your brain cave in with all the freight
of things you are no longer looking for.

One quick crack

One quick crack on the edge of time
And the soul slips into the blades of the whisk
Songs for sugar
Dreams for fat
Bones for flour
And poets left to tongue the bowl.

But half a sonnet

I peg my lady's smalls out on the line
Clandestinely alternate with mine

How seemly yet lubricious this
Suspended parable of bliss

O blow you winds and intertwine
Her littleness engrossed in mine—

And let it rain from time to time

Centenary

10.45 p.m. August 4th

Hesitant the single bell tolls through the dark
as if a wounded soul crawled through the mud
no longer knowing right from wrong or where
lies home. The cars and motorbikes roar by
the World moves briskly on. In Gaza
as the last post sounds another salvo lands
another rocket soars and heads of States
stand side by side in retrospect
throwing up their soiled hands.

Our Glorious past

So what is it now barely a week?
Looking back a few thousands
dead in Belgium
Gaza or could it be Iraq?
Back home bowed heads
grand hullabaloo
and seemly ceremonial
in yawning August sun
and Nature groaning
let's get this done—fast-forward
clouds scream over
rain lashes down and look

it's like November
the bitter wind detaches
bunting as the faux
historic trenches
fill up with mud
devoid of bodies—
Nature yelling now
Will that do you—how many
millions do you need?

Well you know what they say
ignore Nature
sooner or later it goes away

The summer we've had
we can't complain
and the football season
is under way
swings and roundabouts
and know what
it's nice not being in Rio
watching the Germans
winning again we've
got a new Doctor Who'll
see us right and it won't be long
till Scotland's gone or not
whatever and what shall we do
with those Union flags
hanging like wet rags there
in the senseless rain?

Kingdom Come

Uncradle-Methodist I stand
blatant in my tennis gear

the pavement being wide
they pass with nod and smile

him in the sort of suit
I label Finchley Road

from the late Thatcher years
her emphatic in a frock

emboldened with great
smacks of carmine flowers

watching their backs I see them
taking hands for all the world

like Startrite kids clean shod
and firmly on the road

scarcely aware the blood
the World in all its damnable

blind works shall have to wade
its bridling horses through

Pencil on a piece of string

Let's see what trail the dream-fox left
lurching from cover in the chill night air
the shops are close the pavements broad
and slippery with blood ? Well yes.
The sun shines bright those clouds
are gone that loomed as close
as sniff in that strange evening air.

The quiet radio in the corner of his bed
against the wall is telling how all
prisoners must have the vote
(a pencil on a piece of string)
or compensation at the least—
and what to do with such access of right?
Which politician should he murder first

to earn his term (that death for sure
already justified)? Have not those foxes
pencilled in the guns and bombs to send
about the world? Next time online
he'll tick them off—Democracy's fruits
the shops are close the pavements broad
and slippery with blood ? Well yes—

Making an exhibition

At the turn of the Town Hall stairs we pause
to take in the display, the clever childrens-book
allure of posters shining on the walls—
WOMEN OF ENGLAND SAY GO the best/the worst.

I wonder did the Beastly Hun address
their young with such assurance and finesse,
or were things different there, your Prussians
all with polished boots and ready for the off?

At the head of the stairs a lady of about our age,
dressed in the part, smiles welcome, points
to the papers on her desk *Will you enlist?* Bang
to rights my wife explodes *Certainly not—that's*

an appalling idea. We leave the poor dear hanging
on her own barbed wire, feebly murmuring,
That's not very patriotic. Poor lass—she dressed-up
nicely for the day, got in the spirit of the thing

and here we are behaving just as if the whole shebang
were real. It's all so *very* long ago. Why so stand-offish,
so abrupt? We don't look mad, yet stalk the well disposed
displays as if we smelled the piss, the rotting flesh.

A lesson remembered

waiting for poetry competition results

The post has not yet come the dustcart
roars and clatters down the road as yet.

It's as it went when throwing pots
waking early feeling great to make a start

you'd wedge and weigh a ball of clay more
than your wheel could take and somehow centre it

then plunge your fist into its heart
and knuckle it to clumsy life and collar it

with forearms and locked hands
and feel it rising like a monstrous thing

which as your leg pumps up and down
you pull into a proud and sentient grace

the wheel thumps on as proudly you lean back
to sponge and wet your hands before

you deftly close the neck into a bottle
or a dome—and watch it suddenly collapse—

that silly second when you thought how good
then felt the clippers take your wings—

post nemesis you throw a dozen
mundane pots none of which to be ashamed

the post brings catalogues for shoes and clothes
a tax code and some minor bills.

Morning song

In the cane sofa lugged from the tip
I lean back to chat to the early sun

a touch embarrassed by the marks
on the glass of the garden doors

though the sun's not bothering—
straight in over the quarries across

that nice kelim that *will be the death of us*
and over the real ash planked floor

to highlight my worn slip-ons still
dirt encrusted thick from replanting

the bulbs of the lilies (who neither toil
nor spin) turned from their broken and

unmended pot into the dark unfettered
earth the climate here in this our cluttered

final spot being kind to lilies and
old bones though as I scribble this

the leg crossed-over's going numb
and the shoulder groans at push of pen

as moment by sweet moment I allow
the dust-spored kiss of the gypsy sun.

Night sweats

Perhaps it's guilt he wakes some nights
to scent of burning or of blood and flowers.
It's not as if there's much to fright or fret
to raise his body heat and yet he burns

safe in his cosy little nest above the hum
of traffic and the first slight song of birds—
being not troubled by a kicked-in door
a shell a rocket or a helicopter bomb

the soft dry kiss of poison gas (he pays
protection against all such). See how he fills
a box with cans of beans and soup
accepts no change from the Big Issue guy

a standing order with Amnesty and Centrepoint
for not a lot it's true (they Gift Aid everything)
and please— they did work hard enough
and chanced their arm to end up in this place.

It's only what they both deserved and yet
the cold sweat pearls across his waking face
the pain he cannot share subsumes his pain
his nights too long his days too short.
Fact is he's been too cowardly to trouble life
so why that thump between the ribs—the knife?

Triangle of forces

Patience a virtue not given to seagulls
I wish I could tell this immaculate
brigand (probably last year's
scruffy squab) that pears take time
that working such bounty loose
does no one good – take unripe
fruit and a brutal beak all you get
is what sailors say of a bar of soap
given a squeeze between strong fingers
off it shoots and leaves you eyeing
pears on flagstones down below
too close to doors and windows
for even the boldest pirate's reach.
Bugger-off I shout but quietly not
wanting to wake old-fashioned
neighbours or alarm the wife but
there behind me in the doorway
she's telling me I will not win
and anyway those pears are useless
scabby at best. She indicates the jars sat
on the shelf above her head as yet
untried and yes as usual she's right.
The one jar sampled strangely
reeked of balsawood cement—
I tell her *there's a principle's at stake*
our tree our fruit our yard our waste.
She shakes her head and turns indoors
but her thought bubble clearly says
his chimney his nest his air his roof.

Our mark

and come the storms
what steps reveal themselves
made by some future primitive
when Time has ducked us
on our heads and washed
our little words away

between the surf and suck
what have we done
what now sits rounded in the hand
what edges still can cut and scar?
Oh yes our mark is everywhere

despite the sea has perfect skin
looked at from now and here
and yet the isles of plastic grow
the algae bloom and rendered
blind by noise mechanical
the sapient whale gasps
on the beach beside its calf

the waters climb into the sky
the shelf on which our quick
world sits breaks off
drifts slowly South—
a white bear howls

Good paint

His daughter thinks it needs another coat
he thinks it all looks fine
Bearing in mind the Planet their pockets
they scavenge at the tip for cast-off paint

she'd rather just fork out but
lets him have his way
two flights up in the flat they carefully unlid
and mix their little bits of brilliant white

she overcomes her doubts
he's pleased as punch
one half a can of masonry luscious
as crème fraîche topped up with all the rest—

She's busy worrying he won't approve
her letting to the two disabled boys
he's thinking a full five litres free
but now they find that as they try it out

he loves the goodness of her heart
he asks what if they flood the bath
solid chunks of West Bay cliff donate stiff
blobs which bloom as ochre flowers?

with tenants such as these he asks
will she be still insured she sighs
he knew there had to be a reason why
you buy a tub of new and start again

on his say so she takes expert advice that
tells her no—sadly she tells them so
a let-out then to do your less than kind
to turn away and paint it over white.

Night-night my little darling

Ibuprofen/ Scotch to help me sleep
I creak towards my bed almost amused
how old I feel how joints and muscles
tell me I should crawl there on all fours
age is no time for dignity and yet
I'm up like lightning to swat
that darling fly with nearest book to hand.

Merwin's *Shadow of Sirius* does the job
to the manner born—take that—poetry's
effects both various and great delivering
death immediate and yet somehow vicarious—
I say a fevered prayer no daft old blundering
Deity this moment reaches for a book
of favourite and effective poems.

Mental shrug

It's no good expecting things just to go right.
Steer well clear is my advice
recork your hopes pickle your dreams

keep your distaste to yourself
eat your leftovers
change your socks— well once a week.

Speaking personally we've done our best—
not put a foot wrong
not poked at the hornet's nest.

Look at us now still standing well back
eyes barely open sweet
music trickling in our ears.

Okay somewhere there may be screaming
untoward things happening
it's no good chasing the ambulance.

Personally I'm not money-minded. So fold
your arms with luck you can get through it
knowing it was nothing *you* did that blew it.

Mother-daughter

As in the mirror
that looks in the mirror
that looks in the mirror

so it must be for the mother
watching her daughter
put up her long hair

though to the viewer
seeing the girl in her
bright bloom of beauty

it occurs to stay the
sculptor's hand
stop now you might say

yet seeing the mother
life's carving upon her
it catches the breath—

the beauty to be
still unbelieving
still unbelieving

Press any key

My wife sits softly swearing at the screen.
Love of my life, I think, press any key you
still are beautiful and look at you that
thing you curse ten years ago
you wouldn't give the time of day
scribing in your peerless hand those
blissful letters I have always been
too proximate to personally receive—
believing as you did (perhaps still do)
that this black shallow box will steal the soul
from out the breast as soon as look at you.
I bring you coffee with a stealthy tread.

Having just exited our Tax Return online
I sympathise but steer well clear—
the anger we both feel with this our
tick-box world is easier to unload on near
and dear than on these dead yet vital things
that lie so many fathoms deep in our
crashed ignorance. Experts will come—
our daughter chief among. She will swim
down and though she may not fetch our pride
alive will comfort us, seek to explain just why
we came to grief as we sit numb and dumb—
survivors yet still ticking primed to blow.

I sit as far as possible in the same room
pretending to ignore you with my book
but look at you. Repeatedly you stab
the keyboard, tense, intent as a seagull

chasing chips in a pebbled beach. I want
to bring you paper and a pen but since
your wrist that's not so easy now. Now
is now—and that sweet girl was then.
Press any key my love. Begin again.

Insight

Look says the Angel throwing a fist
of my poems into the air *it's easy*
I watch them falling flakes
of large snow onto the grit
of the Autumn pavement
melting away

down on my knees and scrabbling
I hear the laughter
of wings flensing the air

is it blood from my fingers or
my poems bleeding?
Whatever the pavement lies
gleaming
silver-red as sunset

now there's an insight
calls the Angel
suddenly wistful

but put on some gloves
before you start typing

Plea

Look I say to the trees
there is really no hurry
though you are tired of green
see how the night rain
has touched-up the colour

no need yet for change
for trying on yellows
and orange and brown
for shedding your clothes
for winter sleeping

so do not listen
to swallows in rows
on wires those twittering
émigrés they are
no loss let them go

lithe though you are
you cannot follow their
flit across water and sand—
here comes the skipping wind
go on—hold out your hands

Whose Angel are you?

You worry too much, says the Angel.
His profile tilts to the backwash wind
like that superior hunting dog
whose name as ever escapes me—
What is it I say what is it now—
I'm smelling the coal the steam
there's nothing like it—

whose Angel are you anyway?

All I've missed is a poem I say
it's not the last train. He smirks
and sighs (an ineffable combo)
Yes, and knowing you, there's another
one through in a minute! You've been
talking to Cope again I mutter
you know I don't like it—

whose Angel are you anyway?

We can't all be successful, he smiles,
though you try I grant you—
I don't make cocoa for anyone I tell him
or hang around waiting for buses—
arctics now—look here's another—
if you're quick you could throw
yourself under.

I don't need this

Take it from me says the Angel *love is haemophiliac*
bleed— bleed—bless you—if that was a sneeze?

You know about bloody love then I snort.
I thought 'love was a strictly a human problem'?

I'm only trying to help sighs the Angel *if you could stop*
picking your teeth for a minute I could tell you how

it's going to be. So many times I've seen it O so many
I see my Angel weeps and wish I could hold him

comfort him—*not me you poor fool* he snaps mantling
it's you whose dreams will soon be ash— your woman gone

or her left alone when all that is hers for the keeping
is this bloody stack of verse and shoes—or say by

some miracle you manage a cliff or a car crash.
I don't need this—we'll get through it somehow.

Don't give me that yells the Angel thrashing the warm
stale air to an icy blur *imbecile don't you know that*

while you sit scribbling the flower in your hand is fading
and God knows no garden there to hide in?

How to kill a good man

A Jehadi song

He will be your message
and your messenger
and this his last good offering.

Do not forget he is your enemy
although he cannot fight
because his hands are tied.

Remember now he speaks for us.
For their contempt
our father Abraham demands his death

and blessed be his Holy Name
our God has sent a lamb.
Hold up your blade against the sun.

The sacrifice deserves no less—
a clean blade and a steady hand
no hint of light along the edge.

People who can't compromise

for both mothers

Like every mother's son he played with knives
the menfolk laughed and told us not to fuss—
and they were right he soon grew out of it
grew in its place this conscience thing—and I for one

was glad aware the playground bullying.
I never thought it could end up like this
I thought he would do better in the world.
He's been away all sorts of places now for years

Now you tell us those who know they're right
who know there's something they must do
who cannot come to compromise will be
The death of us—every mother's son.

Symbiosis

So it has always been
since the first stone-axe—
men have tortured trees
butchered them
for their likely limbs
torched them to points
hardened to murder
made them accomplice—
how the bears still scream
from the cracks
in the pavements

So children playing in parks
move on from the hearts
scarred into the bark
by long-dead lovers
leaning tiptoe to reach
innocent fingers
into the almost human faces
cupped in the swollen lips
the tender callous of mouth
that at a whim
might bite

Pretend

Gently as dandruff the years drift down
O hoover away
the shoulders get heavy with used up skin
O brush and shake
it's harder and harder to keep awake
O wouldn't you say
it's harder and harder to get to sleep
O come the day
weird as tumbleweed thoughts roll by
O wouldn't you know
you're way off the map you knew as a kid
O for pity's sake
you're alive in the great grey yonder of age
O wouldn't you know?

No—I am two in the summer grass
O crawling away
wet arsed with the buttercups in my face

Forbidden fruit

We note the shuffle of dead leaves
the tree of sensibility is bare. Deciduous.
While blooming youth's so evergreen

and snakes turncoat in Paradise
not tempting us but saying no
to things not good for us. Ridiculous.

No longer up to climbing trees
we step the little ladder of our days
and dare ourselves to lean

beyond the wobble of our legs
to fall into the bramble bush—
O sugar the berries in the pan.

When they get home our legs
beside themselves season
into planks of pain. We dignify

ourselves on nice firm chairs to watch
the youthful dancers on the screen
and sit and lignify a little more

and wish our parents were still here
to tell us sweets are bad for us
and have we washed behind our ears?

We cannot hear them for the noise of
council workmen blowing leaves
beneath the parked cars in the street.

Rude awakening

What? What is it for godsake, I say?
Come on, says the Angel, *you've got*
to see this. He's dragging me, bedclothes
and all to the landing. What is it? What's
going on—it's barely morning? *The sky—*
look at that sky! Eyes barely open still
I can see what he means—the heaven's
a floating silk scarf of mother-of-pearl, hints
of heavenly duck-egg showing through.
Yes, I agree, He does a good sky, your
old Gaffer—*not Him,* squeaks the Angel,
us! We've been trying our hand at filo pastry—
we're going on Bake-Off—there's three layers
up there, thin as you like. Old blue eyes
won't know what's hit him—can't wait to see
sweet Mary's face. Mind you, we have cheated
a bit—well, not cheating really, just flew
a few Jumbos round for an hour, blew all
the dust from those air-strikes into signature
feathers—what do you think? I'm impressed
I offer. *I know what you're thinking, he sighs,*
it was better before the blood dispersed,
richer, stronger, know what I mean?

From Mr. Weston's Book of Household Management

I put the kettle on and think what next?
You need an extra hand to ease the black bag
past the wire-loop handles from the bin.
They tell me you should lift the liner out
and then it's simple—simpler at least but
something in me wants to do the job
the way I've always done the thing.

Wrong-headed and persistent I proceed.
A corner of a carton snags and tears the bag
odd bits of rubbish strew the floor. Pride
undented I twist and tie the neck of it
and find the dust pan and the brush
and sweeping up think how I should
first put a new bag in of course too late.

I leave the loaded pan down on the floor
and snap one from the roll and feed it in
having at last undone its sly resistance
to presenting any sort of opening. I lift
the handles up and feed the edges underneath—
and one foot on the pedal—turn to pick the pan up
off the floor—and kick it hard against the door.

Love watching

Love watching these things, don't you?
When the nights draw in, when you draw
the curtains not for the sun but for the cose,
once you're through the weather and the News
and close-up with Attenborough
or the Deadly 60 gang—mind-blowing
the photography—you feel not so much
voyeur as god come down in human guise
to lean against a wide rib-footed tree
or hang suspended in the glorious canopy
to see the adolescent males with whoops
and yells beat the shit out of the weakest one
and throw him from the group—now they are gone
the camera closes in on the poor thing's
bloody whimpering—clearly not long to live—
leaves you shaking in your chair to think
how far we human beings might have come.

Scottish Wednesday

Old leaves blown-in out of the Autumn wind
we plump on the chairs at the side of the hall
to lace on our shoes to ask how we are
but when our travelling steps are checked
once our strathspey lines have kissed the floor
when we've walked it through and the music begins
what are we then but young girls and young men?

What are we then but young men and young girls?
so raise a cheer to this level place where Time
learns how to set to one corner and then to another
and feels the tug of a firm old fist and   whatever
his blunders we carry Time laughing through it
though men are not always men but shoulder a band
to circle like true men hand in hand.

Lemons in a bag

He liberates the lemons from their yellow string vest
as always marvelling how they roll from the knife
like adolescent breasts

not that he's ever been given to such wonders
seeing as he is the middle of three
well brought-up brothers

and then again how the vest itself reminds him of his dad
when he was getting very old sat there on the edge
of his lonely bed

and saying I'm in trouble son parting his legs to show
how the heparin has blown his balls up like balloons
that was supposed

to help the blood-flow up his neck so he regained
the balance he had always had—soon after
he complained

his feet were cold
soon after
he was dead—

knife in hand he hesitates
blade kissing the yellow skinned
grenade

Eyewash

When the Moon's on its back like a puppy
enticing the sun to play
when the clouds standing-off in the corners
might possibly go either way

when the magpies laugh in the bushes
too many too clever to count
then on with a boot and a sandal
open the door and step out—

your foot on the pavement may change it
into fabulous gold
or you slip on some delicate dogshit
and come-to in a neighbour's hall

and maybe he's never spoken
and maybe you've never smiled
or wanted to be beholden
and you don't like the way it's tiled—

but Life has an eye for weakness
and Time is the Dog that passed by—
so as he is tending your grazes
gaze deep in your neighbour's eye

Earwash

Won't be a tick he calls rinsing the syringe
the one without a needle not so far used
refilling printer cartridges and mixing
handwash with warm straight from the tap
he thinks he should have eased the wax
with olive-oil plugged in with cotton-wool
but they are out of oil and cotton-wool
he wouldn't have the first clue where to look—
not here in their new place—he can recall
exactly where it used to live back there
although those nearly fifty years have gone
like pavings overgrown—he reaches in
from time to time to pick the blackberries
the sharp green apples hiding in the leaves
to bake and crumble—words for winter days
and yet no actual sense of having been there still
remains except sometimes in dreams he'll find
himself up on a roof relaying tiles on battens
that are shot his ear pressed to the pillow
for dear life and in the morning waking
to roof-fall in the tunnels of his ear and
nothing but the far-off knock of blood—
and so because he does not wish to wait in line
for some kind nurse to ream this orifice he fills
and squirts and wipes the wet-warm from his neck
and hopes he won't regret the simple act—and hears
her calling from downstairs and though he'd like
to do it all once more knows he had better go—
they both catch less these days than lovers should.

A nod in passing

Living where we do close by the church
we may suppose some simple norms—
the men who ride each day with death
have decent fingernails though not perhaps
as perfect as those boxed and flowered away
in limos waxed and buffed to blaze of black
a sudden flash of morning sun now all dissolved
to grey soft swish of tyres along the littered street—
a brief stare from a pallid bearer in the back
as if to say he's passed me by— just for today.

Alright for some—look at the old fool
elasticated at the knee racket in hand
embarrassed I dare say to see the likes of me
off to do a decent day—doesn't know the half—
these cars don't get to look this way by squeaking
through the toytown brushes down at Morrisons
oh no it's roll your sleeves up time—they used
to send these Yops to try the work—that streaky lot
could no more clean a wheel hub than their ears
old Eddie used to say down on your knees boy
shine until you fucking see the goofy teeth of Death.

Vegetarian section

Feeling bored
feeling his gruff charm slipping away
he cut out his cold grey heart
and put in its place a half
beetroot (boiled)—

instead of his grey tired eyes
he popped in one black olive
one green (the pits squeezed out)
he crammed his sore old feet into
fresh banana-skins
and began to dance—

from pitted eyes he watched
the local Ladies Circle
(Vegetarian Section)
giggling like carnivorous
schoolgirls shyly advancing
to tear him apart

Shoe song

He counts the pairs of shoes he has—
they lie about his floor like feral cats.
The room must smell but he is used to this.

He sighs and moves a pair from fist to fist.
Downstairs he thinks he only has two hats
and counts again the pairs of shoes he has

their size increasing with the years—
he can remember when a ten would fit
(the room must smell but he is used to this)

elevens calmly came and went—the bliss
of twelves their lack of willingness to hurt.
He counts again the pairs of shoes he has

still wears the extra-extra wide—he'll miss
them now brash thirteens rule the roost.
He counts the pairs of shoes he has—
the room must smell but he is used to this.

I hear you

I hear you at the linen basket rummaging
thinking a wash worth managing
and maybe so—I let it go—
you'd not be told.

The cutpurse wind drops now and runs for France
the plucked trees view their leaves askance
strewing pavements and parked cars
with stolen gold.

Beyond Colmer Hill, to the West-North-West,
the sky strips bare to show its manly chest
and pulls fresh clouds from the Irish Sea
clean and cold.

Past days we've had our moments of high wind
swept now into the corners of the mind—
such waste of energy such hours
of sulk and scold.

Yet now the sky is blue and full of fluffy lambs
and perfect life may be a sham—
a shambles yes but from the slaughter
laughter, love unfold.

Drop everything

Drop everything says the Angel *come with me*
not much to drop—I'm in the shower.
He drags me by the ear my hair not long enough
out through the velux into Autumn air
and dangles me ridiculously there.

It's Market Day. Far off the Sally Army plays
no doubt folk fumble for their souls
and if they're lucky find enough loose change.
What if they all look up I ask? He grins
only saints look up he says *what they divine*

defies all commonsense—I'd say you're safe
if safe is what you want to be? A passing seagull
blesses us—it teflons through the Angel onto me.
What are we doing here? My ear hurts— I'll
catch my death. *You're almost dry now—save your breath*

listen and look—your culture— everything you love
the dreary hand-me-downs not one thing done
in all your days that has not been already bought
and sold a thousand times and still you sluice your skin
and step into your shoes the soul of you worn thin.

Aren't you ashamed to be such waste of time and space?
Hold on I gasp. *Is this unfair?You don't agree?*
I'm slipping I yell! *Not yet* he says *you are not yet*
for Hell. I feel his nails dig in. What must I do?
Not for me to say old man—the next bit's up to you.

Incongruity

He reads the works of poets who have come and gone
the works of poets who have come and come
the works of poets who have caught the gravy train

he hears the shaman chanting in the wood
watches the boys who spray the walls
he feels the spatter of wrecked brains

to none of these does he belong but picks up
letters in the street and rescues from night motorways
the metaphors squealed out of speeding cars—

but most he Prufrocks on with coffee and with tea—
he stares the hairs along the arm too stiff
to roll his trousers to the knee—

and yet and yet he's walking to the post
with envelopes addressed to Poetry Prize
as if he simply cannot see the stamp of incongruity

What's wrong with poems?

I get to the door before they bang again—
I've probably lost my place on the page.

Don't you ever put any air in the tyre?
says the Angel, looking quite out of breath.

Falling back, I tell him, trust you to come in
wheeling that—who said you could borrow

it anyway? *You do it,* he says, *it's all stuff*
you're needing. He lets go the handles,

steps away from the barrow and pushes in by.
I've half a mind to leave it on the street

but I turn it round and wheel the damn thing in
and out at the back. It's beginning to rain.

I open the shed and start to unload—he smirks.
Two bags of quicksetting Resentment,

a damaged bag of old fashioned Grit,
a collapsible shovel, the sort for digging

a tunnel, a pair of old gloves, a rusty trowel!
I thought, says the Angel, *we might make a start?*

The Bunker, he says, *your Mausoleum? No bricks*
but what's wrong with wodges of poems?

To make a little something

November sees my window bare of words
sadly so—a bitterness I would not share.
The chill of failure in the air yet the sun laughs
Spring. Forget-me-nots and roses still sparkling
the grey stone of our little yard. Feigning,
we cling by fingertips to what we were
knowing the only way is down and how
to make each other laugh and you , at least,
you sensible in only being set on pleasure
failing to understand my stupid need
to make a little something of myself.

To make a little something of myself,
failing to understand my stupid need,
you sensible in only being set on pleasure
to make each other laugh and you, at least,
knowing the only way is down and how
we cling by fingertips to what we were
the grey stone of our little yard feigning
Spring, forget-me-nots and roses still sparkling.
The chill of failure in the air yet the sun laughs
sadly so—a bitterness I would not share.
November sees my window bare of words.

Angel in trouble

Am I missing something? Says the Angel
I don't look up though it's hard to ignore
sevenfoot of feathers at your bedroom window
You're actually smiling at eight in the morning—
What gives? Had a good night, that's all
and I'm not hurting for once. Now please
bugger off— I'm busy. *Just wanted to see how*
we were he smiles *make you a coffee yes?*
After the last time? You've got to be joking.
What are you after? I swing round to face him—
it's the best I can do not to burst out laughing
I am not After I am Before-and-After I am Alpha
and Omega I am the Dancer of needles! That
doesn't explain why your head is a pumpkin
surely that's not your usual style of dancing?
I was caught in the moment he wails *these children*
so dangerous—I only wanted the brats to know how
it would look like alive! Idiot, I tell him, they've
got telly for that. Won't it come off? *Only*
he cries *if someone utterly disbelieves.* I ponder.
If I do that it means you'll be gone and although
you're a positive nuisance I wouldn't want that—
can't you ask Dawkins? *He's no good—can't even*
see me— please— you could at least tell them it's only
a pumpkin—behave like a grown-up—I am your Angel?
Where are they then, I sigh and how many?
They are legion—they are dancing on my feet!

Carwatch

Idly I run my finger round the fascia-shelf
and brush it on the carpet to remove the dust
and wonder should I shake the footmats out
but leave them be leaf-litter stones and all.

I sit and watch the windscreen huff
Half-wishing *I* was ten or so and hitting
balls in the bright November sun.
The boy is best left to correct himself

not helped by whispered shouts from me
to take the hands from out his pockets and
get stuck in. His own worst enemy but
aren't we all? I must just leave it to the coach.

He'll tell his mum that it was good—and then
how something wasn't really fair or
reasonable how his feet hurt and why
can't he just meet his father just the once?

He shuts his mother back in hell. The bars
of love he slams and runs his stick along
are forged of her sweet care. She gave herself—
her dividend this lovely fiend— this not

required-by-daddy child. One day perhaps
he'll realise he softly fell on his sweet butt
into the opened harbour of her arms—was not
flushed out into the big bad world.

Telescope

It stands three-leggèd in the attic
this star-transfixed giraffe so alien
I've not yet fathomed it. Six months
or so since on a whim I shelled out
in the market for the thing thinking
the boy might have some fun with it—
and give him credit he has tried
convinced himself he's seen a star
close-up and personal though when
I look there's nothing but a blur
of birdshit on the velux. The older
the more you're sure of falling short –
a crucial pain (death by a thousand cuts).
We must let someone show us how
before the snowflakes melt and run
from my dear grandson's eyes. Meanwhile
I stroke the damn thing's neck and swing it
gently round then clump downstairs
to make a cup of tea and put things off
and type this up for all the good that does.

Supervision

As he sometimes does he's chuntering on
sotto voce taking me through the catechism
of his latest thing much as my little brother
used to do (still does—come to that). Today it's
Super Heroes with all the tatty salesman's glitzy
chat of special powers—*your turn Grandpa.*
I make one up no less likely than the plethora
the money-men have squeezed like cancers
grown from cells that don't know when to die
sliced and diced in petrie dishes growth-factor
larded-in. I'm rather pleased with Mantis Man
and bless the boy he's ready to believe but draws
the line at Ketchup Man. For now it's real enough
despite I want to tell him look there are none such
no super-heroes only ordinary guys with special
weaknesses for doing stuff far out beyond the call
who almost always come to grief and he should
simply watch his back for pushers on the street
and grow up safe and tall non-competent to fly to see
through walls or rescue anything at all but his own skin
and do his little daily bit of good unseen. So why
as I drive-on, my one good eye fixed on the road,
why am I thinking back to when with an old
a curtain round my neck I whizzed fist-thrust
around the moon far out beyond the stars woolly
wild and all alone and dangerously good as gold?

Curtains for us

What's-cooking-good-looking I ask
then notice the wings or what's left
and the stench of it hits me—burnt feathers

Looks like it's curtains for us you and me both
groans the Angel *fireworks* he sighs
could never resist them— light me a Lucifer!

No I say 'while you've a Lucifer to light
your fag smile boys that's the style'.
Smartarse says the Angel *and I don't do I*

have a Lucifer these days? Just give us a fag—
different back then. Not the bloody Fall again
give it a rest and have I ever smoked?

Not back-then-back-then— the time you humans
had a go—I have to say not bad almost
the real deal—all the lovely charging horses—

then you rolled out the bloody tanks and gas
that's when the fun went out of it—poor
Lucifer it broke his old-school heart

never the same after that—reckon
it's curtains for us you and me both—
the big cream ones from the front room

bring 'em through Fritz— be an angel
wrap me up warm sing me a lullaby
do it nice Tommy do it nice.....

A time to celebrate?

A hundred years on what a killing we've had
what a razzamatazz of remembering how
in the trenches of France the young of Europe
toppled their doppelgang foes in the strictly
come difficult dance of death the breath
sucked out by shell and rolling mustard gas
envelopes-home dispatched at a bloody limp
and oh the pity the pain the desperate wait—
and here we sit to watch our brave boys salute
in the sand seeing back home the good old Queen
bestow a wreath on the powerwashed stone—

then in barely a heartbeat it's the Strictly Results
oh the pity the pain the desperate wait
for the spray-tanned pairs and it isn't fair
who survives who doesn't who never deserved it—
never mind eh? Year after blooming/blossoming
year it goes on— the routines the tricks each time
more inventive the contracts renewed behind
lines behind the closed doors re-jigged to make
money and all of us wishing real war was mere
entertainment all glitter and tears and finally
buried beneath bright poppies in budgeted mud.

Winging the moment

Seagulls rummaging jumble-sale clouds
squabble their finds as
he sits in the car while his grandson hits
with the coach on the court

coffee-in-fist the sweet girl who comes-in
next door asks is he okay
he explains while her dog nuzzles his hand
that the boy is best left and

is wondering how it can be when
the grubbiest squab can fly
tuned to its feathertips—look at this one
the one even now grenadiering by—

instinct with all its wants and needs how
chased by the dog it lifts away
scrap in its beak—winging the moment
supremely sure—so why oh

why not this boy he loves but expects
will stomp furious with failure
having not actually beaten a man with
a lifetime's hard won skill—

this lovely boy dropping the promising
scrap as he scutters sidelong away
from the black dog that harries him
every demanding, difficult day?

Nearly perfect

Ring on/ two eggs/ two bay-leaves in the pan
a little cold the kettle on for topping up—this

morning he might get it right—the headlights
of the sun come up and over Bothen hill

an early walker is consumed by fire
he quite expects to see bright sparks fly up

the eggs are bouncing in the pan he tops
the water up and fills the little cafetière

to slide on when the eggs are done he hears
his wife tread sleepy-eyed across the landing

to the loo and waits the tumbling clump of her
hot-water bottle down the stairs—there—he

goes to fetch but glancing up is captured by
crucified against the light a cyclamen exuding joy.

The eggs as usual over done. He knows
the moment he picks off the shell into the bin.

Ah well—butter three cracker-breads—pretend
the eggs are nearly perfect— as they nearly are.

Staying with us

In our long, thin bathroom this morning
I hear him sing this child of my child.
He's doing a poo and he's singing the wall
on which I have penned in silver and gold
the words of the pencilled scrap we found
the move into the Barn—a card she made
when she was small from her big heart.

As is his way he scats and recomposes it
to make it all his own.

Be—be—careful yeah,
be careful oh yeah—

oh yeah be—because
be careful love—
love—love

yeah I love you

because

www.ingramcontent.com/pod-product-compliance
Ingram Content Group UK Ltd.
Pitfield, Milton Keynes, MK11 3LW, UK
UKHW020239250726
13967UKWH00001B/457